Funerals

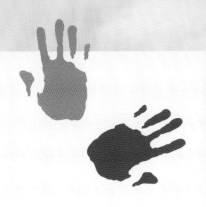

Mandy Ross

Heinemann Library
Chicago, Illinois

© 2004 Heinemann Library
a division of Reed Elsevier Inc.
Chicago, Illinois

Customer Service 888-454-2279
Visit our website at www.heinemannlibrary.com

Designed by David Poole and Geoff Ward
Originated by Ambassador Litho Ltd
Printed in China by Wing King Tong

08 07 06 05 04
10 9 8 7 6 5 4 3 2 1

Library of Congress Cataloging-in-Publication Data

Ross, Mandy.
  Funerals / Mandy Ross.
     p. cm. -- (Rites of passage)
Summary: Explores the origin, historical or religious significance, and practice of funeral ceremonies in different cultures around the world.
Includes bibliographical references and index.
  ISBN 1-4034-3987-7 (lib bdg.) -- ISBN 1-4034-4596-6 (pbk.)
  1. Funeral rites and ceremonies--Juvenile literature. [1. Funeral rites and ceremonies. 2. Rites and ceremonies.] I. Title. II. Series.
  GT3150.R67 2003
  393'.9--dc21
                          2003001897

Acknowledgments
The author and publisher are grateful to the following for permission to reproduce copyright material:
Cover photograph: Corbis/Owen Franken.
p. 4 Terry Vine/Getty Images; pp. 5, 8 Mohamed Ansar/ Impact; p. 6 Richard T. Nowitz/Corbis; p. 7 David Rubinger/ Corbis; p. 9 Thomas Dworzak/ Magnum; p. 10 Wolfgang Kaehler/Corbis; p. 11 Dennis Johnson/Lonely Planet Images; pp. 12, 16, 19 Christine Osborne; p. 13 Rex Features; p. 14 Christopher Bluntzer/Impact; p. 15 Mark Henley/ Impact; pp. 17, 24 Christine Osborne/Alamy; p. 18 Robin Laurance/ Impact; p. 20 Christine Osborne/Syder; p. 21 Najlah Feanny/ Corbis; pp. 22, 23 South American Pictures; p. 25 Philip Gould/Corbis; p. 26 Mark Cator/Impact; p. 27 Harry Gruyaert/Magnum; p. 28 Phil Schermeister/ Corbis; p. 29 Mo Wilson/Photofusion.

Special thanks to both the Interfaith Education Center in Bradford, England, and Georga Godwin for their help in the preparation of this book.

Every effort has been made to contact copyright holders of any material reproduced in this book. Any omissions will be rectified in subsequent printings if notice is given to the publisher.

Some words are shown in bold, **like this.** You can find out what they mean by looking in the glossary.

Contents

Why Do We Have Funerals?

A funeral is a special **ritual** or gathering held when someone dies. It gives relatives and friends a chance to express their love for the person who has died and their sadness at his or her death. After a funeral, a dead person's body is usually either buried underground or **cremated.**

There are two main purposes for a funeral: to take care of the body and the spirit, or **soul,** of the person who has died, and to look after the needs of the living people left behind.

In every culture around the world, funerals and special rituals are carried out when someone dies. Rituals may include washing and dressing a dead person's body, leading a body in a **procession** to the place of **burial** or cremation, and celebrating the life of the person who has died.

Flowers are often put on a coffin to show love for the person who has died.

Rites of passage

In 1909, Arnold van Gennep wrote about rites of passage. He made up this term to mean events that mark important times in a person's life. He said there are three changes in every rite of passage:

- leaving one group,
- moving on to a new stage, and
- joining a new group.

What happens to us after we die?

In some religions, people believe that after death a new life begins in heaven, or close to God. Other religions teach about **reincarnation**—the belief that a dead person's spirit starts a new life within another living being. Some people believe that death is simply the end of life.

These different beliefs affect the traditions for dealing with the body. For example, most people who believe in reincarnation see the body as something that is no longer needed after death. So cremation is used rather than burial.

This is a procession to a funeral in French Guyana, South America.

Jewish Funerals

Jewish funerals take place as soon as possible after someone has died, usually within 24 hours. According to tradition, most **Jews** are buried after they die. Although some Jewish people now choose **cremation** instead.

A dead person's body is washed and dressed in a white **shroud.** The body is placed in a simple coffin—it is the same for everyone, rich or poor. The coffin shows that everyone is equal in the eyes of God. Someone stays with the coffin until the funeral, to show respect for the person who has died.

A rabbi, or Jewish religious leader, says prayers with the family at home before the **burial**. At the burial ground, the rabbi, relatives, and friends say **memorial** prayers and readings from the Hebrew Bible, the Jewish **holy** book. The rabbi speaks about the person who has died, celebrating his or her life and achievements.

*These **Orthodox** Jews are praying around the grave in a Jewish cemetery. An Orthodox Jew is one who follows the laws of Judaism strictly.*

The writing on this gravestone is in Hebrew, the language of Jewish prayer. A gravestone is set up about a year after a death, to mark the end of the year-long time of mourning.

For seven days after a death, the family stays at home to **mourn** the dead person. This is called sitting *shivah*. Relatives and friends visit for prayers every evening. On the anniversary of the death each year, the dead person's name is read at a **synagogue**. Relatives light a special candle, called a *yahrzeit* (YART-site) candle, which burns for 24 hours.

Mandy's story

Mandy, who is Jewish, remembers her uncle's funeral:

Our rabbi led the funeral prayers and talked about how my uncle had been a good man. Afterwards, we sat Shivah at home for him. He had so many friends and relatives, and they all came to celebrate his memory and comfort our family.

Muslim Funerals

When a **Muslim** is dying, he or she will try to say the *shahadah*, a special prayer that declares faith in God, or Allah. When someone has died, it is traditional for Muslims to say, "To Allah we belong and to Him is our return." Both of these sayings show the importance of Allah.

Muslim families are often sad at losing someone they love, but they are comforted by their faith. Muslims believe that if a person has lived his or her life according to Allah's law, his or her **soul** will go to Paradise after death. This belief is expressed in the Qur'an (kor-AN), the Muslim **holy** book.

*These men are carrying a coffin in a funeral **procession** in Pakistan.*

After death, everyone is treated the same, to show that everyone is equal in the eyes of Allah. A dead person's body is washed and then dressed in white cloth. The cloth may have been worn by the person when he or she went on a **pilgrimage,** or *hajj*. The funeral and **burial** are usually held as soon as possible after a person's death. The body is taken in a coffin to a mosque—Muslim place of worship—for prayers. The prayers are usually led by close male relatives or friends.

Muslims bury their dead, rather than **cremate,** because Allah said that humans should not use fire to destroy what He has created. Muslims are buried in Muslim cemeteries, lying on their right side, facing the holy city of Mecca. During their lives, Muslims face this direction when they pray. Family members may come and visit the grave.

*These **mourners** are attending the funeral of a young child in Pakistan.*

Maori Funerals

Maori people live in the country that is now New Zealand. Their **ancestors** lived there for many hundreds of years before the Europeans arrived. According to ancient tradition, Maoris believe that after someone dies, their spirit lives on and is cared for by the spirits of earlier ancestors. Maoris believe that their ancestors' spirits live at the traditional meeting place, called the *marae* (ma-ray). They believe that the spirits watch and take part in tribal meetings, marriages, funerals, and other ceremonies held at the *marae*.

When someone dies, his or her body is perfumed and dressed in fine clothes. Then the body is brought to the *marae*. People gather there to pay their respects to the person who has died. The women of the tribe call to welcome the dead person's spirit and to help it on its journey to meet other spirits. Family and friends wail and cry loudly to express their sorrow—and to be sure that the **soul** of the dead person can hear their grief.

This marae, *or traditional Maori meeting place, is in Rotorua, New Zealand.*

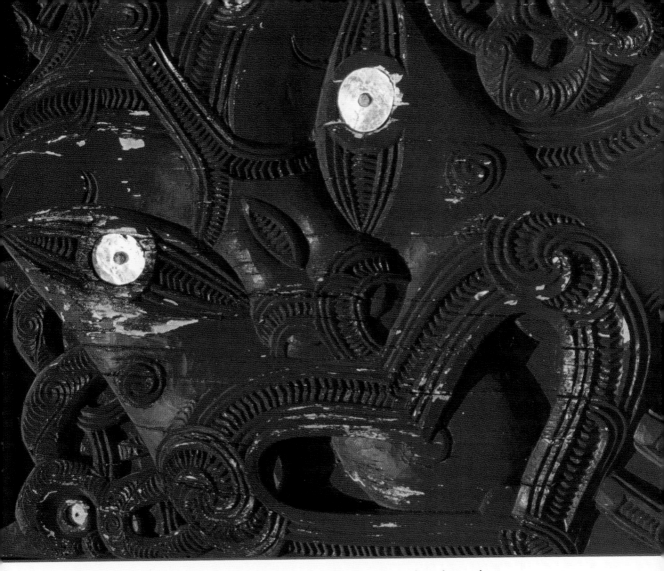

This Maori carving style is called tiki. It is believed to have been carved in memory of an ancestor who died long ago.

On the night before the **burial,** everyone gathers to sing songs and to remember the dead person. They tell stories and look forward to the time when they themselves will meet their loved ones again, after they die.

Then, the dead person's body is buried in the family grave. Afterward, there is a feast for family and friends. The house is blessed so that the dead person's spirit will not hover over it. A **memorial** stone is placed over the grave within five years of the burial.

Christian Funerals

Christians believe that Jesus Christ started a new life in heaven after he died. Thus, they hope that if they lead a good life, their **soul** will also start a new life after death, close to God in heaven. When a Christian is dying, a priest or minister may be called to say last prayers with him or her, to help the soul travel quickly to heaven. A dead person's body is placed in a coffin. Sometimes, relatives or friends watch over it before the funeral.

At the funeral, it is traditional to wear dark clothes. There are prayers and readings from the Bible, the Christian **holy** book, and **hymns** are often sung. Family and friends may talk about their memories of the person who has died and celebrate his or her life.

*This is a traditional funeral **procession** in London, England. The coffin is placed inside the hearse, which is being pulled by horses.*

It is usual for a coffin to be carried into a church or crematorium. Sometimes relatives of the dead person who has died carry the coffin.

Many Christians, especially **Roman Catholics** and **Orthodox** Christians, wish to be buried after they die. If the funeral takes place in a church, then they may be buried in the graveyard beside the church or in a public cemetery.

Other Christians choose to be **cremated** instead. In that case, the funeral is held in a crematorium—where cremation takes place—usually beside a cemetery. After the cremation, the ashes are collected and placed in an **urn.** Some families scatter the ashes later in a favorite place. Others keep the ashes at home or in a special part of a cemetery.

For some Christians, such as Roman Catholics, it is traditional to hold a party just after a funeral, so that family and friends can gather together to celebrate the life of the person who has died. This brings comfort in a sad time. It also reminds the **mourners** that their own lives must continue, despite their grief.

Buddhist Funerals

Buddhists believe in **reincarnation**—that death is the beginning of a new life. A dead person's spirit is born again as another living person or as an animal. Buddhists see death as part of a natural cycle. Many Buddhists choose to be **cremated,** because Buddha, their teacher, was cremated.

*This picture shows a traditional **pyre** for a Buddhist funeral in Bali.*

When a Buddhist dies, his or her body is washed, dressed, and then placed in an open coffin. **Monks** may visit the family to chant from the Buddhist **holy** writings.

The dead person's body is taken in a **procession** to the crematorium, where the cremation takes place. At the funeral there is more chanting, to help the dead person's spirit on its journey. Relatives offer flowers and **incense** to Buddha.

The day after the cremation, the ashes are collected and may be kept in an **urn**. Family and friends gather seven days after death to chant prayers for seven weeks after the death. Buddhists give food and money to the poor and to monks after someone has died. They do the same every year on the anniversary of the person's death.

*People gather for a funeral at a Buddhist **temple** in China.*

Janaki's story

Janaki, a Buddhist from Sri Lanka, remembers attending her grandmother's funeral when she was twelve:

> *My grandmother's body was carried to the cemetery near her home. There, the coffin was placed on a pyre built of bamboo and decorated with coconut leaves and white tissue paper. I was so sad, I cried and cried. But we hoped that her next life would be happy and good.*

Sikh Funerals

Sikhs believe in transmigration. They believe that after a person dies, his or her **soul** passes into another body. The person who has died is **cremated** because Sikhs believe that the soul has no more use for the body.

Funerals are the same for everyone, rich and poor, because everyone is seen as equal within the Sikh religion. A dead person's body is washed and dressed in white. **Baptized** Sikhs wear the Five Ks, the traditional Sikh **symbols:** *kesh* (uncut hair), *kangha* (wooden comb), *kara* (steel bracelet), *kirpan* (symbolic sword), and *kachera* (cotton undershorts). Then, a dead person's body is brought home for family and friends to say goodbye. At home, the family reads from the Sikh **holy** book, the *Siri Guru Granth Sahib* (sir-ee goo-roo gran-th sa-hib).

These Sikhs are saying goodbye to a dead relative in an open coffin.

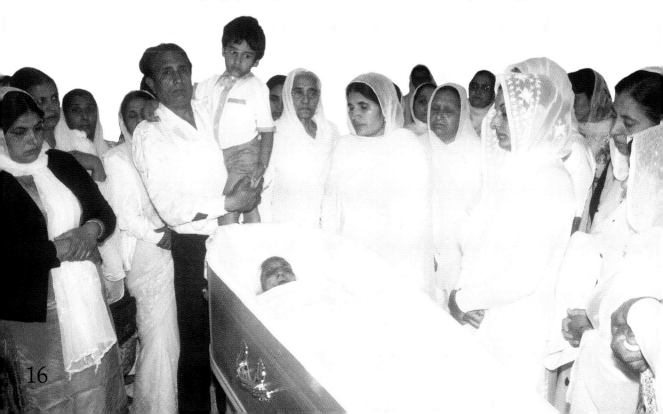

The coffin is taken to the *gurdwara*, the Sikh place of worship. Prayers are said outside the building. Afterward, everyone returns to the *gurdwara* to say more prayers and to share a meal. Sharing food with other Sikhs reminds the family that life must go on. **Mourners** usually give food or money to charity as a mark of respect for the person who has died.

For Sikhs who live in India, a dead person's ashes might be sprinkled in the holy river at Kiratpur in northwest India. Elsewhere in the world, ashes may be sprinkled in a river or the sea.

This is a gurdwara in Great Britain. It is where a coffin is taken and prayers are said.

Hindu Funerals

Hindus believe in **reincarnation**. They do not believe that death is the end of life, but rather the start of a new life. They believe a person's **soul** goes to live within a new living being. So, each person may have thousands of lives in this world. They also believe that if someone has lived a good life, then their next life may be happier.

Because of their belief in reincarnation, Hindus see the body as something that is no longer needed after death. That is why a dead person's body is burned on a fire, called a **pyre,** at a Hindu funeral. Sometimes, the funeral is held at a crematorium. But at a traditional Hindu funeral, pyres are usually built beside a river. They are built near water because Hindus believe that running water is **holy** and cleansing.

The Ganges River in India is considered especially holy. There are pyre sites all along it.

A family scatters ashes into the river at Kiratpur, India.

The funeral usually happens on the same day that the person has died. First, the dead person's body is washed, if possible with water from the Ganges River. Then, it is carried in a **procession** to the place of the pyre.

The dead person's son, or another male relative, walks around the pyre seven times. Then, he lights the fire with a burning torch. A priest chants verses from the holy book, the *Bhagavad Gita* (buh-guh-vud gee-tuh). Relatives and friends say prayers for the dead person's soul as it leaves the body during the fire.

After three days, relatives collect the ashes from the dead person's body. If they can, Hindus scatter the ashes in the Ganges River. If they cannot get there, they may scatter the ashes in a river or the sea in their own country or region.

Air and Sea Burials

Sometimes, **burial** or **cremation** may be difficult or forbidden for religious reasons. Other traditional ways of dealing with a dead person's body include air or sea burials.

Air burials

The **Zoroastrian** (zo-roh-ass-tree-an) religion started more than 2,500 years ago. According to Zoroastrian beliefs, a dead body should not be allowed to touch fire, earth, or water—all of which are believed to be **holy.** Instead, a dead person's body is cut into pieces and left in a high stone tower called a tower of silence, or *dakhma.* There, birds of prey, such as vultures, come for the flesh. Later, the bones are collected.

A similar ancient custom is still used in Tibet. Firewood is scarce in regions of Tibet, and so funeral **pyres** can be very expensive. At dawn, a dead person's body is carried to a remote hillside and left for birds and animals to eat.

Zoroastrians leave dead people's bodies in towers of silence, or dakhma, *such as these in India.*

This funeral service is taking place on a ship. The person who has died will be buried at sea.

Sea burials

If someone dies on a long sea journey, or in a battle at sea, it may not be possible to carry the body back to land. In such cases, a sea burial may be the best option. Some people today choose a sea burial—perhaps if they have enjoyed sailing or vacations near the sea.

For a sea burial, everyone gathers on the deck of a ship. They remember the person who has died and say prayers or sing **hymns** or other songs. Then, there is a respectful silence as the dead person's body is lowered into the sea, inside a **shroud** or coffin.

Remembering the Dead

In Mexico and some other Latin American countries, when someone dies, there is usually a **Roman Catholic** funeral. The person is also remembered on the Day of the Dead. It is a day set aside for the memory of those who have died. The Day of the Dead is celebrated every year on November 2.

The Day of the Dead began many hundreds of years ago in Mexico, before Europeans brought **Christianity** to the people. After the Europeans arrived, many local traditions died out, but the Day of the Dead survived. Today it includes Catholic traditions as well.

People wear costumes and skeleton masks in a procession for the Day of the Dead in Mexico.

In the days leading up to the Day of the Dead, people place flowers and gifts on their family graves. People also leave food and drinks—in case their relatives have grown hungry or thirsty in the grave.

On the day itself, there are large processions to the cemeteries. Families may spend the whole day at their relatives' graves, often bringing a picnic, and saying prayers for the dead.

This stall offers models of skulls and other grave decorations for the Day of the Dead.

Lorena's story

Lorena, a woman from Ecuador, remembers:

My mother died when I was a girl. Every year on November 2, my grandmother prepared avocado, chili sauce, and all my mother's favorite foods. We set out these foods and left the window open all night so that she could come in and eat them. We knew that she did not really come, but it is a way to remember someone who has died.

Dancing at Funerals

In many African countries funerals include music, dancing, and singing. Although relatives are usually sad at the loss of someone they loved, they do not see death as the end of life. Instead, death is celebrated as the way to the world of the spirits. Dancing and music reflect this joyful new beginning. They also help those left behind to express their feelings.

At Yoruba funerals in Nigeria, family and friends dance. They wear **symbolic** wooden masks, and there is drumming, singing, and clapping. According to Yoruba beliefs, a dead person's spirit can still have control over his or her relatives. So, it is very important to carry out the funeral and **burial** properly, in order to keep the spirit happy. Then, the spirit will help the living, instead of haunting them.

These men from the Dogon tribe are dancing on stilts at a funeral in Mali.

When African people were taken by force as slaves to North and South America from the 16th to the 18th centuries, they took their customs with them. Some of these customs still survive today at funerals among people of African heritage in the United States and in Latin America. Often African traditions are combined with **Christian ritual.**

A jazz band plays in a funeral procession in New Orleans, Louisiana.

One example is the jazz funeral, mostly celebrated in New Orleans, Louisiana. Today these funerals are usually held for jazz musicians. A jazz band plays as the coffin is transported in a **procession** to a church. At first, the band plays sad, marching music. Then, there is a Christian funeral service in a church. After the service, the band strikes up a joyous, upbeat sound. Everyone dances their way back to a party given in memory of the person who has died.

Ancestor Worship

In China, as well as Japan, Vietnam, and other countries in Asia, many people still follow the ancient traditions of **ancestor** worship. According to these beliefs, ancestors' spirits live on after death and can affect the living.

In ancestor worship, it is important to treat a dead person's body and spirit with respect at a funeral—and afterward, too. This way, his or her spirit can rest in peace and bring good luck to the members of the family left behind, instead of coming back to haunt them and bring bad luck.

These people are visiting their ancestors' graves in Tokyo, Japan.

These graves are among the rice fields near Hanoi, Vietnam.

At a funeral, **mourners** bring flowers. The body is placed in an open coffin, with the feet facing out. This encourages the dead person's **soul** to leave rather than stay to haunt the living. Family and friends may offer **incense**, candles, tea, wine, and food. Traditionally, everyone gives money to the relatives of the person who has died.

As the coffin is lowered into the grave, everyone turns away because it is considered unlucky to watch the coffin being lowered. Most families spend a month in mourning. Relatives and friends visit them at home, and bring gifts of food.

Visiting ancestors' graves

In China, at the spring festival of *Qingming* (ching-ming), families visit the graves of their ancestors to clean them. They bring picnics, and some of the food is offered to the ancestors in front of the grave. They believe in return, ancestors will bring good health and wealth to the family. Then, the rest of the food is enjoyed by the family.

New and Old Traditions

Many people today do not follow any religion. Their relatives and friends may plan a new kind of funeral without prayers or religious readings. Other people look back to ancient **pagan** traditions that started before **Christianity.**

Pagans hold hands in a circle, surrounded by trees.

Humanists are a group of people who do not pray to a god. They instead focus on the value of human life. Humanist funerals celebrate the memory of the person who has died, and all that he or she did during life, without religious **ritual.** Humanists believe that death is simply the end of life.

According to ancient pagan tradition, trees are a **symbol** of the cycle of life, producing seeds to make new life in a never-ending cycle. Pagans today celebrate funerals among trees or in the woods. They hold hands to make a circle, to symbolize the cycle of life.

Some people choose a green **burial.** This is a burial in a grave marked by planting a tree instead of a gravestone. Over time, the trees grow into woods as a **memorial** for those who have died. More and more green burial grounds are being created, as more people choose this kind of burial.

A decorated cardboard coffin is being used at this green burial in Devon, England.

Myra's story

Myra was an adult when her mother died. Here, she remembers her mother's nonreligious funeral:

When our mother died, we wanted the people who had loved her to lead her funeral. We asked her two dearest friends to speak about her life. Then, my sister and I talked about our memories of her. Another friend chose music that my mother had loved when she was alive. Thinking about what to say at her funeral helped me to appreciate what she had given to us, her family, and friends.

Glossary

ancestor relative in the past. Grandparents and great-grandparents are ancestors.

baptize clean spiritually; give a name to

Buddhist person who follows the way of life taught by Buddha, who lived in ancient India. Buddha was not a god, but a man. He taught his followers how to live simple, peaceful lives, called Buddhism.

burial act of placing a dead person's body in a grave and covering it with earth

Christian person who follows the religion of Christianity, which is based on the teachings of Jesus Christ. Christians believe that Jesus was the Son of God.

cremation burning of a dead person's body

Hindu person who follows Hinduism. Hindus worship one god, called Brahman, in many forms. Hinduism is the main religion in India.

holy special, because it has to do with God or a religious purpose

hymn song in the praise of God

incense substance that gives a sweet smell when burned and is sometimes used in religious rituals

Jew person who follows the religion of Judaism. Jews pray to one god.

memorial way to honor and remember someone who has died

monk member of a monastery, an all-male religious community. Monks devote their lives to God.

mourn feel or express sadness that a person has died

Muslim person who follows the religion of Islam. Muslims pray to one god, whom they call Allah.

orthodox strict or traditional

pagan someone who does not follow any of the major world religions, but instead sees the natural world as holy

pilgrimage journey taken for religious reasons

procession people walking together along a route as part of a public or religious festival

pyre pile of material, such as wood, for burning a dead body

reincarnation belief that after death, each person starts a new life on earth as another living thing

ritual set of actions always done in the same way, often as a religious ceremony

Roman Catholic Christian who follows the leadership of the pope in Rome

shroud light sheet that is wrapped around a dead body before burial

Sikh person who follows the religion of Sikhism, based on the teachings of the ten gurus, or teachers

soul non-physical, spiritual part of a person that some people believe survives after death

symbol when a picture or object stands for something else

synagogue Jewish place of worship

temple building used for worship

urn vase used to store the ashes of a dead person after cremation

Zoroastrian person who follows the religion of Zoroastrianism. They live in India, where they worship one god, and believe that the world is a struggle between good and evil.

More Books to Read

Broadbent, Lynne. *Life's End*. Chicago: Raintree, 2001.

Johnston, Marianne. *Let's Talk about Going to a Funeral*. New York: PowerKids Press, 1997.

Parker, Victoria. *The Ganges and Other Hindu Holy Places*. Chicago: Raintree, 2003.

Pirotta, Saviour. *Christian Festivals*. Chicago: Raintree, 2001.

Index